KEKKAISHI
結界師
2
田辺イエロウ
YELLOW TANABE PRESENTS

The Story Thus Far

Yoshimori Sumimura is a *kekkaishi*, or barrier master, an expert in fighting demons. Currently in his second year at junior high, he is training to become the 22nd kekkaishi in his family line. Each night, he patrols Karasumori, a cursed area that attracts supernatural beings of all sorts and is now the site of Yoshimori's school. This duty has been passed down through his family for generations.

Tokine Yukimura, Yoshimori's next-door neighbor, is also a kekkaishi. The Sumimuras and the Yukimuras have been quarreling for more than 400 years over which family is the legitimate successor to their kekkaishi school.

As a child, Yoshimori made a mistake that caused Tokine to suffer a serious injury. Yoshimori was deeply shaken by this incident. Devoting himself to his training, he promised himself that he would become a strong man and be able to protect Tokine in the future.

KEKKAISHI VOL. 2

TABLE OF CONTENTS

DAD!
Chapter 8: TOKIO YUKIMURA
ARE YOU GOING TO WORK?
TAP
TAP
TAK
I'LL GO WITH YOU.
TOKINE ...
SHF
YOU'RE NOT READY FOR THAT YET.

WHY NOT?
I KNOW THE SPELLS. I CAN DO IT, EASY!
I KNOW.
I KNOW THAT VERY WELL.
YOU'RE VERY GOOD.
IF I WERE A LORD AND YOU WERE MY KEKKAISHI, I'D REWARD YOU RICHLY.
TOO BAD I'M NOT YOUR LORD, HUH?
SEE YOU LATER.
HA HA HA!
DAAAD! WAIT!
I SAID NO REWARD FOR YOU.
I DON'T WANNA REWARD!
I JUST WANNA HELP YOU!
LET ME SHARE MY SECRET WITH YOU.
COME COME
I...
...LOVE YOU SO MUCH.

I'M YOUR FATHER. I CAN'T BEAR TO BRING MY BELOVED CHILD TO THE BATTLEFIELD !!
PAT PAT
SO, AT LEAST UNTIL YOU ENTER JUNIOR HIGH...
...LET ME TAKE CARE OF THIS BUSINESS ALONE.
THE *HOIN* DIDN'T APPEAR ON ME...
...LIKE IT DID ON YOU.
BUT... ...I'LL DO MY BEST.
OKAY?

Chapter 8: Tokio Yukimura

Student Counseling Room
HELLO. LET ME INTRODUCE US TO YOU ONCE AGAIN!
TAA
DA
I'M MYSTERIOUS ENGLISH TEACHER TATSUMI MINO, AND THESE ARE MY FRIENDS.
STARTING FROM MY FAR RIGHT...
ZAM
IN CHARGE OF HEALING...
JOSEPHINE.
IN CHARGE OF DEFENSE...
SIMONE!
ZAM
ZAM
IN CHARGE OF OFFENSE...
ROXANNE!

NOW ALL OF YOU...
BOW!
PAKK
UM... I HOPE ...
...THIS ISN'T WHY YOU MADE US STAY AFTER SCHOOL TODAY.
OF COURSE NOT.
THE FUN IS YET TO BEGIN.
HEE
BEHOLD THE SHOW I HAVE TRAINED THEM TO PERFORM ESPECIALLY FOR YOU!
GET IN LINE.
KLUNK
IS THAT WHAT YOU INVITED US HERE FOR?
DON'T EVER CALL US HERE FOR SUCH A STUPID REASON AGAIN!
GRR
GRR
GRR
WHY ARE YOU ANGRY?

I WAS SO HAPPY.
I'VE NEVER BEFORE MET UNUSUAL PEOPLE...
...LIKE YOU.
AND YOU SAVED MY LIFE!
DIDN'T I PLAY A PART IN SAVING YOU, TOO?
STAY AWAY FROM HER!
THAT'S WHY I'VE PREPARED THIS SHOW FOR YOU.
YEAH
WE'VE REHEARSED SO MUCH OVER THE LAST FEW DAYS, WE'VE HARDLY HAD ANY SLEEP!
COME ON, ROXANNE!
SHALL WE GO HOME?
KLUNK
YEAH.
HE'S NOT REMOTELY LIKE I THOUGHT HE WAS.

HE DOESN'T SEEM TO BE A BAD GUY, THOUGH...
YEAH, YEAH.
HONESTLY, THOUGH, I THOUGHT HE WAS CUTER WHEN HE WAS EVIL.
AND WHY NOT? I LIKE DANGEROUS MEN.
AHEM.
COME TO THINK OF IT...
...BESIDES US, I'VE NEVER MET HUMANS WITH UNUSUAL POWERS BEFORE.
COME ON, CHANGE THE SUBJECT...
HAVE YOU?
WHAT? YEAH.
THE SHADOW ORGANIZATION...
...SOMETIMES HAS MY FAMILY HOST TRAVELING MAGICIANS. YOU KNOW, JUTSUSHAS.
SHADOW ORGANIZATION?
I WONDER IF THAT'S THE SHADOWY RESIDENTS' ASSOCIATION MY GRANDPA MENTIONED.
REALLY?
I DON'T THINK MY FAMILY'S EVER DONE THAT.
OH...
YOUR MOTHER WAS A GREAT JUTSUSHA, BUT SHE KEPT TURNING DOWN THE SHADOW ORGANIZATION'S REQUESTS TO LET OTHER JUTSUSHAS STAY AT YOUR HOUSE.

HOW IS YOUR MOTHER DOING THESE DAYS?
HUH?
I DON'T KNOW. SHE COMES HOME OCCASIONALLY, BUT SHE DOESN'T STAY LONG.
I WAS TOLD SHE'S WORKING AS A KEKKAISHI SOMEWHERE ELSE.
I SEE.
I'M SORRY. WE SHOULDN'T BE TALKING ABOUT THIS AT SCHOOL, DURING THE DAY.
SEE YOU.
HEY!
AREN'T YOU GOING HOME?
I HAVE TO RETURN A BOOK TO THE LIBRARY.
OH.
IN THAT CASE ...
...I'LL WAIT FOR YOU...
...AND WE CAN WALK HOME TOGE--
SHING
SHE'S GONE!

雪村
YOU WERE SENT BY THE SHADOW ORGANIZATION?
NO ONE TOLD US...
...YOU WERE COMING.
THEY DECIDED TO DISPATCH ME AT THE LAST MINUTE.
I'M NOT SURPRISED THAT YOU DOUBT MY STORY.
KYU
HE CAN CLEAR THINGS UP.

ZU
ZU
ZU
I WANTED TO SEND THIS KID AHEAD OF ME...
...BUT HE MOVES TOO SLOWLY.
THIS IS AN OFFICIAL EMERGENCY ASSIGNMENT.
PLEASE ACCEPT IT.
OF COURSE.
BUT PLEASE REFRAIN FROM USING MAGIC ON THE STREETS.
OOO! I'M SORRY.
WHAT WAS I THINKING?

I'M HOME.
RATTA
DO WE HAVE A GUEST?
TOKINE.
HOW DO YOU DO?
MY NAME IS YOMI KASUGA.
I'LL BE STAYING AT YOUR HOUSE FOR A WHILE. NICE TO MEET YOU.
UM.
NICE TO MEET YOU, TOO.
I'M SURPRISED...
...THAT A PRETTY YOUNG GIRL LIKE YOU IS THE DESIGNATED HEAD OF YOUR FAMILY.

WILL YOU BE WORKING IN THIS AREA?
YES.
SINCE MY ASSIGNMENT IS TOP SECRET, I CAN'T PROVIDE DETAILS.
BUT IT'S A SORT OF FIELD RESEARCH. YOU KNOW, CHECKING UP ON MATTERS... THAT SORT OF THING.
JUST BETWEEN US GIRLS, OKAY?
IN ANY EVENT...
...I'VE WANTED TO COME HERE FOR A LONG TIME.
YOUR FATHER WAS VERY KIND TO ME.
DID YOU KNOW MY FATHER?
YES.
HE HAD A LOVELY SMILE...
...AND HE WAS FUN TO BE AROUND.
TOKIO...
...USED TO SMILE AND CHEER ME UP WHEN I WAS DEPRESSED.
I'LL ALWAYS BE GRATEFUL TO HIM FOR THAT...

≡SIGH.≡
IT'S TRULY UNFAIR THAT SUCH A GOOD MAN HAD TO DIE...
...SO VERY YOUNG.
OH, LATER ON I'D LIKE TO BURN INCENSE FOR HIM AT YOUR FAMILY ALTAR, IF IT'S ALL RIGHT WITH YOU.
THUNK
CHK
SHE KNEW MY FATHER...

SHIVER
DAD...
TK
TOKIO!
HONEY! HONEY!
TAKKA
TAKKA
SHUUU
AHH... AHH...
SHIZUE! STOP PANICKING AND GIVE HIM FIRST AID!
DRIP
DRIP

AHH ...
HONEY! HONEY!!
HURRY, SHIZUE!
THOSE ARE THE SUMIMURA'S SHIKIGAMI.
TOKINE, STAY WITH YOUR FATHER!
DASH
YES!
TAK TAK

RATTLE
TMP
TMP
RATTLE
BOOM
I'M SORRY...
...BUT WHEN I GOT THERE, TOKIO WAS ALREADY...
I TERMINATED THE AYAKASHI.
...
I REALLY DON'T UNDER-STAND WHY...
...TOKIO FELT HE HAD TO COMPLETE THE JOB ALL BY HIMSELF...
I'M NOT ABOUT TO THANK YOU!!
SLAM

AH...
AH...
NYA
TOKINE ...
GASP
GRP
WAH!
DON'T EVER...
...LET YOUR GUARD DOWN, OKAY?

Chapter 9
Demon Tamer

TAK TAK
TOKINE!
DETECT ANYTHING UNUSUAL?
NOT REALLY.
HAKUBI IS CHECKING THE BACKYARD NOW.
?
SHE'S ACTING WEIRD TONIGHT.
WHERE'S THE SARCASM?
MADARAO?
WHY DON'T YOU GO ON PATROL, TOO?
WHAT? WHY SHOULD I?
WE CAN SPLIT UP TONIGHT...
YOU GO THERE.
I'LL GO HERE.
CAN'T WE JUST WAIT UNTIL SOMETHING HAPPENS? WITH MY FANTASTIC SENSE OF SMELL, I'LL CATCH WIND OF THE FIRST INTRUDER.
YAWN
...

I SEE... WELL, I ENVY TOKINE FOR HAVING SUCH AN OBEDIENT DOG.
SIGH
HEYY
WAIT JUST A MINUTE! WHICH PART OF ME DO YOU THINK IS INFERIOR TO THAT PUPPY?
WAIT FOR ME THERE! I'LL SNIFF OUT EVERY SINGLE ABNORMALITY..
GRR GRR
SHOOO
...AND FOREIGN OBJECT ON THE SITE!
CHING
DUMB DOG...
TAK TAK
TUP
SHA-TUR
STUP
...
UM...
I BROUGHT ...
...SOME GOOD STUFF TODAY.
GRP

RIGHT NOW I'M INTO CHOCOLATE CAKES.
FUMBLE
FUMBLE
THIS IS STILL AN EXPERIMENT, BUT...
ARE YOU STILL DREAMING ABOUT MAKING CASTLE CAKES?
WHY NOT?
THERE'S NOTHING WRONG WITH THAT!
UM, WHATEVER...
FWIP
ANYWAY, I THINK THIS ONE'S PRETTY GOOD.
SO...
I WANTED TO SHARE IT WITH--
PA-CHING
WE HAVE AN INTRUDER.
CHAK
OF ALL THE...
SHF SHF
SHF

SHA
I BELIEVE IT ENTERED AROUND HERE.
THE ODOR STILL LINGERS HERE, BUT THE EVIL VIBES ARE GONE.
THE INTRUDER MAY HAVE ALREADY LEFT.
SNAP
WHAT?
EEK!
FLOP
THUD
OWW ...
IS THIS MISS YOMI?

NO! IT'S NOT WHAT YOU THINK! THIS SITE ISN'T THE OBJECT OF MY SECRET RESEARCH! ABSOLUTELY NOT!
WHAT ON EARTH ...
DO YOU KNOW HER?
WEIRD LADY!
YEAH ...
SHE'S STAYING WITH US. THE SHADOW ORGANIZATION SENT HER.
SHE'S CUTE! ♡
I'M CARRYING OUT A CONFIDENTIAL ASSIGNMENT...
DOES THAT MEAN SHE HAS SPECIAL POWERS?
WAS SHE THE ONE WHO ALARMED US JUST NOW?
YES, YES! IT WAS MY MAGIC POWERS THAT CAUSED...
AH!
OH, NO NO NO!
IF I WERE A JUTSUSHA, I WOULDN'T VOLUNTARILY DISCLOSE MY TALENT TO OTHERS!
MMMF MMMF
SIIIGH

BY THE WAY, YOUNG MAN...
DO YOU HAPPEN TO BE THE SUMUMURAS' KEKKAISHI?
HUH?
YES...
WOW, I THOUGHT SO!
HELLO! MY NAME IS YOMI KASUGA.
EEK EEK
ER...I'M YOSHIMORI SUMIMURA.
NICE TO MEET YOU.
SO...
...PLEASE DON'T TELL ANYBODY I WAS HERE...
...OKAY?
WILL YOU PROMISE?
ALL RIGHT...
SHE'S WEIRD.
GLEAM
ANYWAY, SINCE WE'RE HERE...
...WHY DON'T WE HAVE TEA TOGETHER?
EVERY-ONE HAS SOMETHING THEY CAN'T LIVE WITHOUT, RIGHT?
FOR ME, IT'S TEA.
I CAN'T LIVE WITHOUT TEA.
GLUG GLUG

I WISH I COULD DRINK FRESHLY BREWED TEA...
SHE EVEN BROUGHT A RUG.
TALK ABOUT PRE-PARED!
...BUT SINCE I TRAVEL A LOT, I'VE HAD TO SATISFY MYSELF WITH OLD TEA IN A CANTEEN.
AND CUPS, TOO.
WHY DON'T YOU TAKE OUT THAT CHOCOLATE CAKE?
WHAT?
WOW.
IT'S REALLY DELICIOUS!
IT'S A BIT AWKWARD TO HAVE A WESTERN DESSERT WITH JAPANESE TEA.
OH.
IT'S OKAY.
I WANT YOMI'S TEA, TOO.
PANT PANT
WAG WAG
SHE ATE MY CAKE.
SIGH... I GUESS I SHOULD BE GLAD SHE LIKED IT.
SLURP
UM... EXCUSE ME...
...BUT WILL YOU BE THE SUMIMURA FAMILY'S 22ND...?
ER, YES.
NOT THAT I WANT TO BE...

I SEE...
YOU KNOW, I KNEW TOKIO VERY WELL.
IS THAT SO?
YES.
BUT I'M NOT...
...REALLY ACQUAINT-ED WITH YOUR FAMILY.
YOU SEE...
...I'M NOT REALLY IN YOUR FAMILY'S LEAGUE.
TOKIO WAS VERY KIND TO ME.
OH, I SEE...

CHIRP
CHIRP
TAK
TAK
TAK
TAK
TAK
TAK
TAK
TAK
STOP FOLLOW-ING ME!
I KEEP TELLING YOU, WE'RE GOING IN THE SAME DIRECTION!
TAK
TAK
HEY, IS THAT KASUGA LADY STAYING WITH YOU FOR A WHILE?
HER?
SHE TOLD ME SHE WAS SUPPOSED TO COM-PLETE HER ASSIGNMENT IN TEN DAYS.
IT'S NONE OF YOUR BUSINESS, IS IT?
DASH
HEY!
...

YOSHI-MORI! YOSHI-MORI!
TAH TAH
HEY HEY
WHERE'S TOKINE?
SHE HASN'T COME HOME...
HUH?
I DON'T THINK SHE'S HERE YET.
HMM.
IN RETURN FOR THAT DELICIOUS CAKE, I BROUGHT YOU SOME TASTY JAPANESE SWEETS.
TEE HEE
HOW ABOUT TEA FOR TWO, THEN?
FINE.
I HAVE SOMETHING I WANT TO TALK TO YOU ABOUT.
AREN'T THEY PRETTY?
THEY'RE SO PERFECT, I ALMOST HESITATE TO EAT THEM.
...

UM... IT'S ABOUT TOKINE.
COULD YOU PLEASE STOP...
...TALKING ABOUT HER FATHER IN HER PRESENCE?
HUH?
ER...
I'M NOT SAYING THERE'S ANYTHING WRONG WITH TALKING ABOUT HER FATHER.
TOKINE'S VERY PROUD OF HIM.
SHE'S DEVOTED TO HER WORK BECAUSE HER FATHER WAS SO DEDICATED.
BUT I WORRY THAT SOMETIMES SHE PUSHES HERSELF TOO HARD.
AND...

I WAS TOO SMALL TO REMEMBER IT, BUT HER FATHER DIED A VERY VIOLENT DEATH.
FROM WHAT I'VE HEARD, TOKINE WAS RIGHT THERE.
WHEN YOU MENTION HIM...
...I THINK IT DREDGES UP PAINFUL MEMORIES.
...
...TRY YOUR TEA AND SWEETS.
UM. I'LL...
YOU'RE SUCH ...
...A SWEET PERSON.
GRAND-MA!
雪村
DO YOU KNOW WHERE MY TENKETSU IS?
WHAT ?
IT WASN'T WHERE I USUALLY KEEP IT.
THAT'S STRANGE. DON'T WE HAVE A SPARE IN THE WARE-HOUSE?

HOW CAN THIS SWEET, GENTLE BOY BE HEIR TO THE SUMIMURAS?
THE WORLD IS TRULY UNFAIR.
WHAT ON EARTH ARE YOU?
SKRUK
KLUNK
IT'S OKAY, YOKI.
COME ON OUT.
SQUIIK

GRM
GRM
GRM
A DEMON ...
GRR
WHIRR

AN INTRUDER!
AND A BIG ONE...
LET'S HURRY, HAKUBI!
DAH
ALL RIGHT, HONEY!
DAH
THAT WAY.
DAH
DAH
CRAASH
WHAT?!
KLINK
UGH...

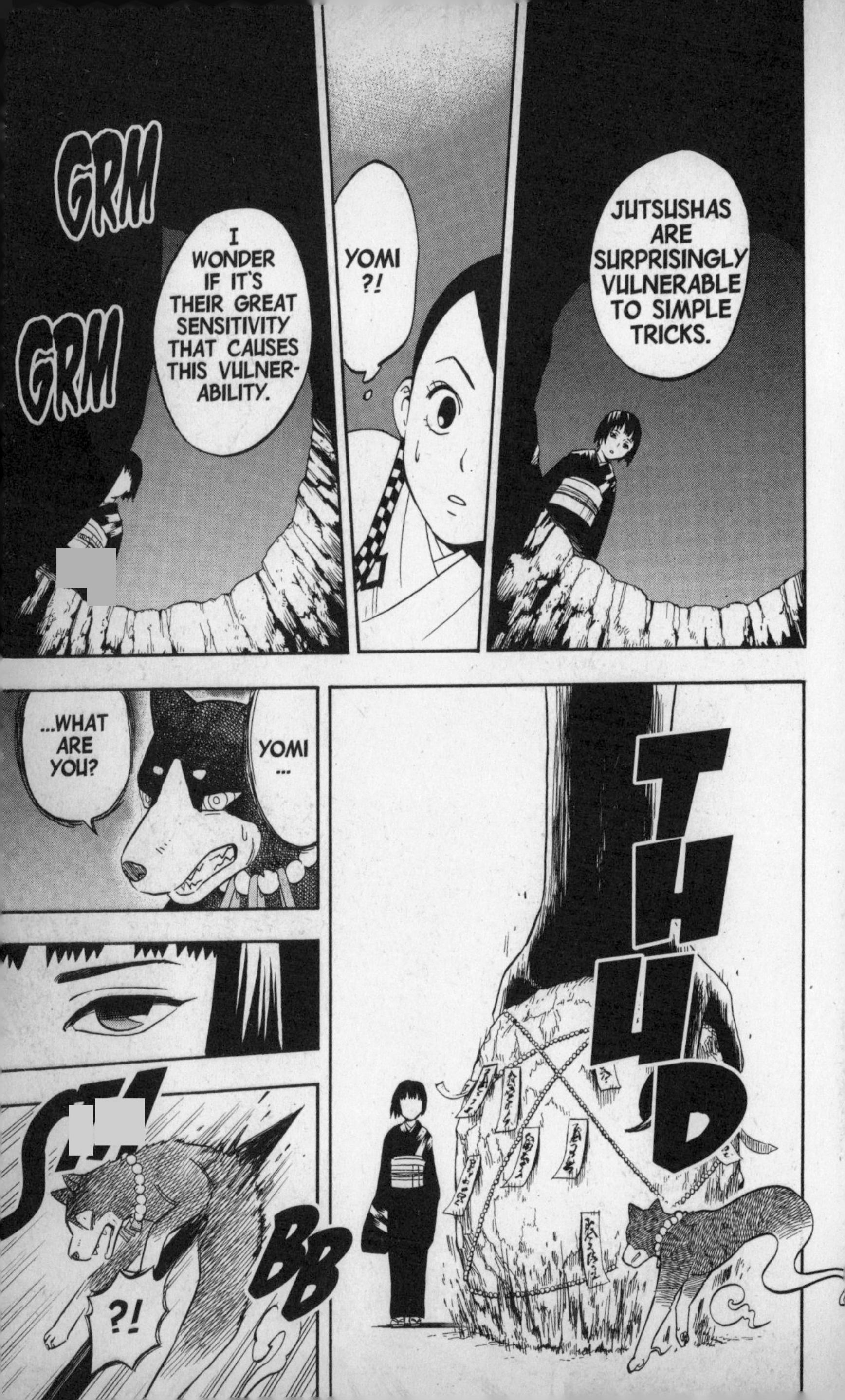

JUTSUSHAS ARE SURPRISINGLY VULNERABLE TO SIMPLE TRICKS.
YOMI ?!
GRM
GRM
I WONDER IF IT'S THEIR GREAT SENSITIVITY THAT CAUSES THIS VULNER-ABILITY.
THUD
YOMI ...
...WHAT ARE YOU?
BB
?!

WRIGGLE
WRIGGLE
NYAA
RA
I, DEMON-TAMER YOMI KASUGA, AM GOING TO TAKE OVER KARASUMORI!

結界師

CHAPTER 10
MEMORIES AND HATRED

RAAAAAA
LET ME GO!
WRIGGLE
YOU... YOU...
WRIGGLE
WRIGGLE
SHOOOO
CREAK

GRAAA
AAAUGH!
GRP
GRP
GRP
AAUGH!
HAKUBI ?!
KLUNK
KLUNK
HAKUBI !
I CAN'T MOVE THIS THING AN INCH!
THE ROCK SITTING ON THIS HOLE MUST BE HUGE.
CRUNCH
HSSSW
...

YOMI!
THIS DOG EVAPORATED IN MY MOUTH, TOO.
HMM.
I WONDER IF THOSE DOGS...
...KEEP THEIR REAL BODIES SOMEWHERE ELSE.
IT'S OKAY.
SHF
YOU DON'T NEED TO EAT THE DOGS.
YOU CAN GROW STRONGER JUST BY BEING AT THIS SITE...
...YOKI.
LET'S CONQUER THIS PLACE.
REALLY?
REALLY.
IF WE DO, I'LL BE ABLE TO RUN FASTER?
SURE.
I'LL BE SMARTER, TOO?
SURE.
THAT'S RIGHT. NOBODY...
...WILL MAKE FUN OF YOU AGAIN.

I SEE...
HEY!
WHAT DID YOU DO TO HAKUBI?!
KLUNK
KLUNK
I WON'T TELL!
BUT DON'T WORRY.
I HAVEN'T FORGOTTEN ABOUT YOU.
AS LONG AS YOU DON'T GET IN MY WAY...
...I WON'T KILL YOU.
OH, DEAR.
SZZ
SZZ
SZZ
SZZ
SZZ
SZZ

WHOOOOOSH
KETSU !!
SHING
IT WON'T WORK.
I SEALED THE ROCK WITH CHARMS TO WARD OFF MAGICAL POWER.
BOOM BOOM BOOM
?!
BAAAN!
WRRR

SHA
TAK
A DEMON!
AND IT'S POWERFUL...
HMPH. SHE TUNNELED SIDEWAYS...
DAH
DA
!
YOKI!

FWAP
STAB
BOOM
YOU CLEVER LITTLE THING.
I TOLD YOU I WOULDN'T KILL YOU IF YOU DIDN'T INTERFERE.
SHE USED SHIKIGAMI MAGIC TO CREATE A MESSENGER BIRD.
BUT NO ONE WILL COME TO HELP HER UNLESS HER MESSAGE IS RECEIVED.
I DON'T NEED YOU.
I HAVE ANOTHER HOSTAGE.
!!

WE DON'T ...
...NEED THAT GIRL.
WHAM
KLUNK
GRR
KA KLINK
WHAT ...
...DID YOU DO WITH YOSHIMORI?
TEE HEE...
DON'T WORRY. HE'S BEEN TUCKED AWAY IN A SAFE PLACE.
I NEED TO BE CAUTIOUS IN APPROACHING THE SUMIMURAS.
I CAN USE THAT BOY TO GET CLOSE TO THEM.

GYAAH
DESTROYING THE YUKIMURAS, HOWEVER...
WHAM
...WILL BE EASY. ONCE YOU'RE OUT OF THE WAY...
...THAT BEAT-UP OLD BAG WILL BE THE ONLY MEMBER OF THE FAMILY LEFT TO HANDLE.
I NEVER THOUGHT I'D HAVE MUCH TROUBLE CONQUERING THIS PLACE, BUT I'M SURPRISED BY HOW EASY IT IS.
SQUIK
SQUIK
I ONLY WISH I'D COME HERE SOONER.
I'M ASKING YOU WHAT YOU'VE DONE WITH YOSHIMORI!
TSK.
EVERYBODY'S WORRYING...
...ABOUT SOMEBODY ELSE. WHY DON'T YOU WORRY ABOUT YOURSELVES?
RUMMMMMMBLEE
UGH!
SQUEAK

K
AH
WHERE AM I?
YOU DON'T GIVE UP, DO YOU?
I'M FED UP WITH YOU...
SQUIK
SQUIK
WHY DON'T YOU BEG FOR YOUR LIFE?
ARE YOU PUTTING UP A FIGHT BECAUSE THIS WAS YOUR DEAD DADDY'S JOB?
IF THAT'S SO, IT'S NON-SENSE.
LET ME TELL YOU ONE THING.

I DETESTED...
...YOUR FATHER.
HE WAS A PATHETIC JUTSUSHA.
HE WAS ONLY ASSIGNED TO PROTECT THIS SITE BECAUSE OF HIS FANCY BLOOD-LINE.
IT WAS OBVIOUS FROM THE START THAT HE COULDN'T HANDLE IT.
AS ANTICIPATED, THE JOB WAS TOO MUCH FOR HIM.
I LAUGHED.
HE SHOULDN'T HAVE FORGOTTEN WHAT HE REALLY WAS.
...
STOP IT...
MY FATHER DID ALL HE COULD FOR US.
DON'T BELITTLE HIM LIKE THAT...
AWW. HE DID HIS BEST, DID HE?
BUT A WELL-MEANING WEAKLING IS STILL A WEAKLING.

THAT DOPE.
SMILING AND SMILING, NO MATTER HOW MUCH THE OTHERS MADE FUN OF HIM.
SO USELESS!
HE WAS WEAK, AND HE SHOULD HAVE ACCEPTED HIS WEAKNESS.
WHAT WAS THE POINT OF DYING SO YOUNG?
HE DIED IN VAIN.
HE DIED FOR NOTHING.
HE DIDN'T DIE IN V--
SQUEAK
THUD
!!
THIS ISN'T GOOD ...
THIS DEMON IS GROWING STRONGER.
SQUIK
UGH...
SQUIK SQUIK
SQUIK
DAD!
SQUIK

SQUASH HER NOW.
FLIK
YOMI.
BOOM
MY...
MY BACK...

GRRRRRRR
WHAM
DA DAK
HYOO
CHA

TAK
CHA CHAK
PING
METSU !!
GRMM
MM
EEK!
?!
YOSHI-MORI ?!
OW... OWW... OWW.
ARE YOU OKAY, YOKI?
TOK

TAKE BACK WHAT YOU JUST SAID ABOUT HIS DEATH.
WHY?
HMPH-- YOU DON'T KNOW ANYTHING ABOUT--
NO, I DON'T.
BUT...
...HER DAD FOUGHT HARD TO PROTECT THOSE HE LOVED.
HIS DEATH WASN'T USELESS BY ANY MEANS.

Chapter 11:
Promise
I'LL GIVE YOU A NAME.
YOKI!
YOU'RE MY DEMON, SO I'LL CALL YOU YOKI! "NIGHT DEVIL"!
ARE YOU...
...SURE YOU WANT ME? I'M SLOW AND...
...NOT VERY SMART.
I WANT YOU!
YOKI IS YOMI'S DEMON. MY GOOD STRONG DEMON!
KEE
REALLY TRULY?

Chapter 11: Promise

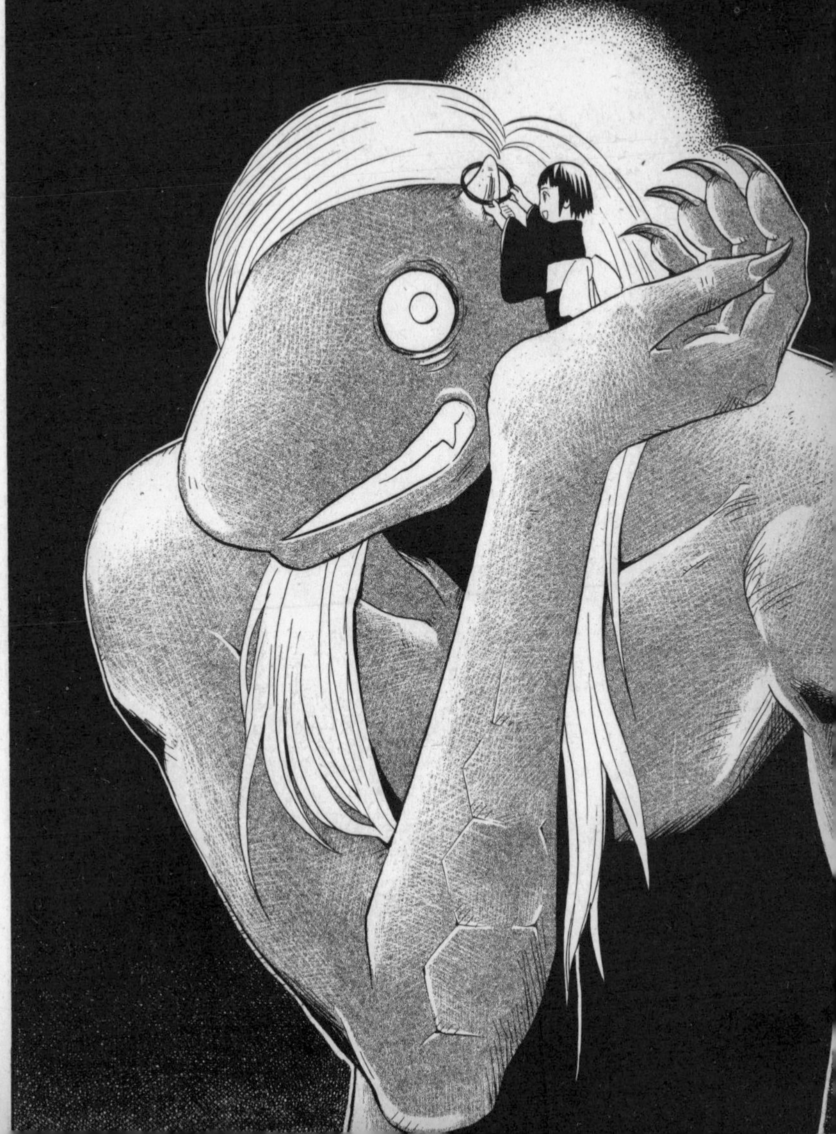

RR
RR
YOSHI-MORI...
I'M SURE I DRUGGED HIS FOOD ENOUGH.
HE CAN'T POSSIBLY HAVE AWAKENED THIS SOON.
WHAT A PEST...
APOLO-GIZE TO HER...

IT MUST REALLY BE HIS DESTINY TO PATROL THIS SITE...
...THEN LEAVE, AND TAKE YOUR DEMON WITH YOU.
DO IT, AND I'LL FORGIVE WHAT YOU'VE DONE TO ME.
I SEE ...
I BLEW IT.
I SHOULD'VE KILLED HIM.
FLIK
WHIRR
WAH!

DAK
DAK
DAK
DAK
WHAT THE HECK WAS THAT?
THUD
SHUUU
ER...
MMF
OH, PLEASE.
!
ASSESS THE SITUATION BEFORE YOU JUMP INTO BATTLE.

TOKINE!
ARE YOU OKAY?
YOU'RE NOT HURT?
I'M FINE.
I SEE.
WHEW.
...
HOW ABOUT YOU?
I'M FINE!
SHE JUST TIED ME UP.
I SEE...
I'VE SPENT TOO MUCH ENERGY.
I CAN'T KEEP FIGHT-ING MUCH LONGER.
WE'D BETTER GET THIS OVER WITH NOW.
LET ME EXPLAIN THIS TO YOU VERY QUICKLY.
JUST NOW, YOU WERE ALMOST HIT WITH THE DEMON'S TAIL.
HIS TACTIC IS TO PIN HIS OPPONENT WITH HIS TAIL AND SQUASH THEM BENEATH HIS HUGE BODY.
THE TAIL IS QUICK, BUT THE BODY MOVES SLOWLY.
I HATE ASKING YOU TO DO THIS, ESPECIALLY AFTER YOU'VE RESCUED ME ONCE...
...BUT YOU'RE THE ONLY ONE OF US WHO CAN CARRY ON THE FIGHT...
...

GOT IT.
SO WHAT DO YOU WANT ME TO DO?
YOU HAVE A PLAN, RIGHT?
GRIN
OKAY.
THE DEMON ACTS UNDER THAT WOMAN'S INSTRUCTION.
I WANT YOU TO DEAL WITH THE DEMON.
WHILE YOU'RE DOING THAT...
...I'LL HANDLE THE WOMAN.
OKAY.

YOKI, CAN YOU MOVE?
Y... YEAH ...
SQUIK
SLITHER
SLITHER
SQUIK SQUIK
!
WOW. I DID IT.
ZAM
IT'S AMAZ-ING...
HE HEALS SO MUCH MORE QUICKLY HERE...

WE CAN DO IT!
THIS SITE IS WORKING IN OUR FAVOR!
WHAT? HE'S ALREADY RECOVERED?
ZAA
WELL.
IT JUST MAKES THIS BATTLE MORE INTER-ESTING.
HMPH.
YOU LITTLE BRAT.
WHRRRRR
YA!
HA!
HO!
WAP
WAP
WAP WAP
LIKE TOKINE SAID, THE TAIL MOVES FAST...
...BUT READING ITS MOVE-MENTS ISN'T HARD, SINCE IT'S CONNECTED TO THE BODY.

KETSU
!
VM
MM
METSU
!!
BOOO
OOM
UGH...
SHUU
WAHHH...
TAK
GYU
SLI
III
THER
HE HEALS SO QUICKLY
!
DRAT
!

HE'S TOO BIG TO ENCLOSE IN ONE KEKKAI...
ZAN
...DESTROYING HIM BIT BY BIT WON'T WORK, EITHER...
...BUT DESTROYING THE DEMON ISN'T OUR MAIN GOAL!
SHUU
MM
VM
FOR NOW...
...TRIPPING HIM WILL DO THE TRICK!!
METSU!!
BOOOM

TILT
EEK--
THUD
THUNK
OW...
CHK
DON'T MOVE.

ORDER YOUR DEMON TO STOP FIGHTING AND LEAVE HERE IMMEDIATELY.
SHUFF
...
YOMI!
YOMI!
AND IF I REFUSE?
LET ME SEE...
I DON'T REALLY WANT TO DO IT...
...BUT I'LL HAVE TO TAKE YOU HOSTAGE.
I SEE...
?!

ZWAM
YOMI.
HOW ...
HOW COULD HE KNOW WHERE WE WERE?
GRP
BAM
EEK!
DASH
THUK
RUSTLE
UGH.
HOW SILLY!
DIDN'T YOU KNOW THAT DEMON-TAMERS CAN COMMUNICATE WITH THEIR DEMONS...
...WITHOUT SPEAKING ALOUD?

THAT'S RIGHT.
WE DEMON-TAMERS SELECT COMPATIBLE DEMONS, NAME THEM, PROVIDE MAGIC TOOLS TO COMMUNICATE WITH THEM, AND SIGN A CONTRACT WITH EACH OF THEM.
YOKI AND I PLEDGED THAT WE'D NEVER BETRAY EACH OTHER.
YOKI?
YOU CAN DO THIS, RIGHT?
YEAH.
THIS BAD BOY IS THE ONLY DEMON I'VE BEEN ABLE TO SIGN A CONTRACT WITH.
THEREFORE, IT'S CRUCIAL THAT I MAKE HIM STRONG.
BOOOM
WHY DON'T YOU GIVE UP?
YOU WANT TO BE KILLED?
LEAVE THIS PLACE!
THIS SITE IS TOO MUCH FOR YOU TO HANDLE!!

...
YOU'LL NEVER ...
...UNDER-STAND THIS.
?!
GO FOR IT, YOKI!
ALL RIGHT!
BECAUSE WE'RE SO CLOSE...
...I CAN FEEL HOW PAINFUL LIFE HAS BEEN FOR HIM.
YOUR DEMON IS SO SLOW!
BIRDS OF A FEATHER, EH?
HA HA
WHY DID YOU CHOOSE THAT DEMON?
YOU'RE NOT MUCH OF A JUTSUSHA TO BEGIN WITH; SO YOU SHOULD HAVE CHOSEN MUCH BETTER.

IT'S NOT YOUR FAULT, YOMI.
IT'S BECAUSE I'M WEAK.
I'LL WORK HARD TO BECOME STRONGER.
PLEASE DON'T CRY...
THAT'S RIGHT.
WHAM
OOPS!
ONLY I KNOW...
...HOW DESPERATELY HE WANTS TO BE POWERFUL!
YOKI!
AT THIS SITE, YOU'LL BE ABLE TO GROW STRONG!

WHAM
WAH!
THUD
ZAM
ZAM
HE'S GROWN MORE TAILS?!
TAH
TAH
TAH
I GOT IT.

SPROING
WHAT ?!
WAAAHHHHHH!
WAP WAP WAP WAP WAP WAP
HE'S CHANGING TOO QUICKLY!
I GOT IT.
INCREASE THE NUMBER OF STRONG PARTS.
DECREASE THE NUMBER OF WEAK PARTS.
IS IT BECAUSE HE WAS SO BIG TO START WITH? OR IS IT...
BUT THE BALANCE IS IMPORTANT, TOO.
ADDING TOO MUCH CAN BE A PROBLEM.
I ONLY NEED THINGS IN THE RIGHT AMOUNT...
...

MY BODY IS TOO BIG...
KRAK
THAT'S WHY I CAN'T MOVE FAST...
BE STRONG... BE FAST...
SQUIK
SQUIK
GET RID OF THE EXCESS...
EXCESS...
SQUIK
FANTASTIC! YOU'RE FANTASTIC, YOKI!
I SEE...
I DON'T...
...NEED YOU ANYMORE.

WHAT?
SNAAP
SMACK
YOKI...
WHY?
YOKI...

BAM
THUD
HE'S NOT WHO HE USED TO BE!
HE NO LONGER HEARS YOUR VOICE...
HYOOOOOOOO

TAK TAK TAK TAK TAK TAK TAK TAK TAK TAK TAK TAK
Chapter 12: Yoshimori vs. Yoki
TAK TAK TAK TAK TAK TAK
IT SEEMS...
...THINGS HAVE TAKEN A TURN FOR THE WORSE.
...
WE'RE SORRY. OUR DELAYED ARRIVAL HAS CAUSED--
BAH.
WE'RE RESPONSIBLE FOR WHAT HAPPENS ON OUR TERRITORY.
SHUDADADA
WAIT!!
SUMI-MURA!
HMP!
WHAT DO YOU WANT, OLD FOOL?
HOW CAN I FAIL TO ACT WHEN THERE'S TROUBLE AT OUR LORD'S SITE?

HOOOOOOOO
CHAPTER 12:
YOSHIMORI VS. YOKI

SQUIK
SQUIK
SQUEAK
IF I ATTACK NOW, I STILL HAVE A CHANCE.
TOKINE, WATCH THIS WOMAN!
OKAY.
GRAB
DON'T... GET IN HIS WAY...
DON'T GET IN HIS WAY!

...
I'M SORRY ...
..BUT I CAN'T LET THAT DEMON GO.
BUT I WON'T KILL IT...
...IF YOU THINK...
...THAT THE DEMON IS IMPORTANT TO YOU.
DAH
...
YOU THINK HE'S STUPID, RIGHT?
BELIEVE IT OR NOT...
...HE'S SERIOUS.

HMPH.
I DON'T WANT PITY FROM KIDS LIKE YOU.
I DON'T PITY YOU.
PERSON-ALLY...
...I THINK WE SHOULD KILL YOUR DEMON.
BUT ...
...THAT'S HOW YOSHIMORI IS.
SHF
THE DEMON HAS BECOME MUCH SMALLER ...
MAYBE I CAN ENCLOSE HIM NOW...
HOI!
WHIRR
JOSO !
SHOOP
SS SS SS SS
?!

FYOO
GRAB
KLANK
HYO
OOOO
OOOOO
THIS IS GREAT.

BA
AH
DAK
HYOO
HE'S FAST!
SHF SHF SHF SHF SHF
SHF SHF SHF SHF
...
GYAH
?!
DADOOM
DOOM
WHAT THE HECK IS HE DOING?
DAH
SHOOP

SHF
WHA
AM
SHOOO
DOOM
KLANK
WHAT ?!
CRM
CRM
IS HE TRYING TO DESTROY THE SCHOOL ?
CRUM
CRUM
...
THIS IS GREAT!
IS THIS ME?
IS THIS REALLY ME?

TOK
I WANT TO CONFIRM ONE THING.
ARE YOU THE GUARDIAN OF THIS PLACE?
...
THAT'S RIGHT.

WHAT A WONDERFUL PLACE.
IT EVEN PROVIDES AN OPPONENT ON WHOM TO TEST MY STRENGTH.
SMAACK
TINNNG
BAM BAM BAM BAM BAM
YOSHIMORI...
...

YOKI!
USE THE ROCK!
SHA
GRAK
BYUUN
GRP
SWIFF
?!
DOOOM

RRUMMMMBLE
...
I SEE.
THE ROCK IS SEALED WITH CHARMS.
HOW ...
...BORING.
IT'S THE KIND OF CHEAP TRICK...
...A WEAKLING WOULD USE.
ISN'T IT?
YOMI ...
...
IT'S OKAY, YOKI...
IT'S BECAUSE YOU'VE GROWN SO STRONG ...
GRR

HMPH.
YOU HAVEN'T EVEN DESTROYED MY KEKKAI.
ARE YOU JUST GOING TO DEFEND YOURSELF?
YOU'RE BORING, TOO.
PING
...YOU NO LONGER NEED ME!
...
OKAY.
WOBBLE
WHY DON'T YOU PROVE...
...YOU CAN DO THAT?
BAM BAM
HE MOVES TOO FAST FOR ME TO THROW A KEKKAI.
THAT MEANS...
BAM BAM BAM BAM BAM BAM
BOOOM

IT'S NOW OR NEVER!!
KETSU!!
WHaAA
AH
BOING
SHFF
SHFF SHFF
SLP
HEY, DON'T MOVE.
YOUR HEAD MIGHT GET BLOWN OFF.

I THINK YOU'D BETTER...
...DO WHAT I TELL YOU.
BAM
HEH. HEH HEH.
I SEE...
SOUNDS LIKE FUN, TWERP!
THAK THAK THAK THAK
THAK
WAIT! STOP!
THAK THAK
THAK
YOU THINK I CAN'T BREAK YOUR LITTLE KEKKAI?
GIVE ME...
THAK
THAK THAK
THAT'S RIGHT ...
GIVE ME...
...POWER!

RR
MORE POWER!!
RIP
RIP
RRAAAW
UGH!
THAT'S AMAZING. HE'S STILL TRANS-FORMING?!
RRIP
THU
WHAT?!
OH...

AAAAAAAAAAAAAAWR
HEY!
YOU!
...
HE'S TRANSFORMING HIMSELF TOO QUICKLY.
HIS BODY CAN'T TAKE ANY MORE...
WHAT?
OH, NO...
HE'S BEEN TRYING TOO HARD...
RAAWR
YOKI...
PLIP PLIP
RRIP
YOKI!
RAAAWR
I'LL GET STRONG FOR YOU, YOMI...
I'M GOING TO TRY MY BEST TO BE STRONG.
YOKI...
WHIR
MOON BLADE!!

ZA
AAAA
WHA'N
THE SHADOW ORGANIZATION!

AH...
SHUUU
CHAPTER 13: SHADOW ORGANIZATION
WHO ARE YOU GUYS?

Chapter 13: Shadow Organization
WE ARE FROM THE NIGHT TROOPS.
WE'RE HERE BY ORDER OF THE SHADOW ORGANIZATION TO ARREST THE DEFECTOR YOMI KASUGA.
Ohdo (Yellow Path)
Members of the "Night Troops," the shadow organization's task force.
Hakudo (White Path)

RAWRRR
RRIP
SQUIK
SQUIK
HMPH. YOU MONSTER.
STILL TRYING TO RESTORE YOUR-SELF?
WHIRRR
MOON BLADE!
WHIRR

SLAA
ASH
THUDD
STOP!
WAIT A MINUTE!
WHO DO YOU THINK YOU--
WHRR
MOON BLADE!
WAHH!
UK
SL

YOKI ...
PLIP
PLUP
YOMI.
SLUP
YOMI.
YO...
...MI...
AHHHHH!!
OHDO.

FWOOOOOM
SUN FLARE BALL!!
THINK THIS IS ENOUGH, HAKUDO?
GO FOR IT.
WHIRR
WHATEVER THAT IS, IT LOOKS DANGER-OUS!!
SHF
FWAH

SHOOOOM
CRACKLE
SORRY TO TROUBLE YOU...
...BUT WOULD YOU MIND FINISHING UP?
ZHAK
TENKETSU!!

GOOOOM

FWOOOOO

TAH
GRAB
...
I'M SORRY ...
IT'S MY FAULT...
I'M SORRY...
I'M SORRY...
I'M SORRY...
...YOKI!!
SORRY FOR THE TROUBLE.

PLEASE LEAVE IT TO US TO DEAL WITH THIS WOMAN. SHE'LL BE PUT ON TRIAL.
SHE'S VERY SKILLED AT LYING AND DECEIT.
WE HAVE NO IDEA HOW SHE FORGED THE OFFICIAL ORDER SHE SHOWED YOU.
WE SHOULD HAVE FOUND OUT WHAT SHE HAD DONE...
...LONG BEFORE YOU CON-TACTED US.
WE ARE TRULY SORRY ABOUT THIS INCI-DENT.
DON'T BE.
I ASKED YOU ABOUT HER BECAUSE SHE CONCERNED ME.
I WASN'T GOING TO PURSUE THE MATTER ...
...AS LONG AS WE DIDN'T HAVE A PROBLEM.
AT ANY RATE...
...HIGH OFFICIALS...
...FROM OUR ORGANIZA-TION MAY PAY YOU A VISIT SOON.
THEY SEEM TO HAVE A LOT OF INTEREST ...
KINDLY REMEMBER THAT.

THERE'S NO DOUBT IT'S DANGER-OUS...
...BUT IT LOOKS LIKE A VERY INTERESTING PLACE, TOO.
PLEASE EXCUSE US.
MAY I SAY A FEW WORDS FIRST?
EVEN IF THEY ARE VIPS OF THE SHADOW ORGANIZA-TION...
...IF THEY EVER ATTEMPT TO DESECRATE THIS SITE, WE WILL USE ALL OF OUR RESOURCES TO PROTECT IT.
KINDLY REMEMBER THAT.

DON'T WORRY. THEY'LL SHOW UP WITH CANDY AND FLOWERS.
HA HA HA
HURRY UP.
STUPID WOMAN.
COULDN'T YOU SEE YOUR MONSTER HAD LIMITS NO MATTER HOW HARD YOU TRIED TO STRENGTHEN HIM?
...
EXCUSE ME!
TAK TAK
PSST
I KNOW I'M NOT SUPPOSED TO HAVE SPARED HIM, BUT...
SWUP

YOKI...
JUST A MINUTE.
IT JUST ...
SQUEAK
...
OH.

CHAK
WOBBLE
IT'S AMAZING! HE'S SO TINY, BUT HE'S ALREADY RESTORED HIMSELF!
TRIP
OH, BUT...
...HE MAY NOT BE ABLE TO GROW BIG AND STRONG ANYMORE.
YO...
...MI.

YO...
...MI.
YOMI!
AFTER ALL YOU'VE DONE FOR THAT MONSTER?
...
I MEANT IT WHEN I TOLD YOU...
...THAT I DESPISED YOUR FATHER.

HE REMINDED ME OF MYSELF.
WE WERE WEAK, BUT WE DID ALL WE COULD TO PROTECT THOSE WE LOVED.
BUT WE'RE BOTH LOSERS AFTER ALL.
YOUR FATHER DIED, AND I FAILED YOKI...
I DON'T THINK...
...MY FATHER WAS A LOSER.
I'M TRULY GRATEFUL TO HIM...
...FOR FIGHTING FOR US TO THE END.
ARE YOU ?
I HID YOUR BELONGINGS AT THE RIVERBANK OUTSIDE THE BACK GATE.
YOU'LL FIND THEM THERE.
...

YOSHI-MORI.
THANKS FOR HELPING ME TODAY.
I REALLY APPRECI-ATE IT.
SHALL WE...
...CLEAN UP THIS MESS?

CHAPTER 14:
THAT'S ALL

YOSHI-MORI!
YOSHI-MORI!
YOSHI-MORI!
MNN.
YOSHI-MORI!
YOSHI-MORI!
SHAKE
SHAKE
OH, IT'S YOU, DAD...
PLEASE, JUST A LITTLE LONGER... I FOUGHT A BIG GUY LAST NIGHT, AND THE CLEANUP TOOK FOREVER...
ARRGH
*THIS KEKKAI IS PITCHED ONLY TO KEEP GRANDPA AWAY, SO YOSHIMORI'S FATHER CAN GET IN.
I'M SORRY.
I KNOW YOU'RE TIRED FROM WORK, BUT...
...I CAN'T PUT UP WITH THIS.
AND I HAVE TO PREPARE BREAKFAST.
COULD YOU STOP THEM FOR ME, YOSHI-MORI?

BAH!
OLD BAG!
HO-HO
STUPID OLD MAN!
KLIK
HMPH!
KER
SPLA ASH
HO HO HO!
HOW RUDE!
YOU EVIL HAG!
KER SPLASH
OLD PEOPLE GET UP SO EARLY IN THE MORNING.
EVEN AFTER STAYING UP LATE LAST NIGHT...

HO!
HA!
HA!
SPLASH
SPLASH
SPLASH
FOOL!
I CAN EASILY ANTICIPATE YOUR MOVES!
WA HA HA HA HA
CUT IT OUT.
SMACK
UGH!
WHAT ARE YOU DOING OUT HERE HALF-NAKED, FIRST THING IN THE MORNING?
I WAS HAVING A RUBDOWN WHEN THE OLD BAG STARTED SPLASHING WATER ALL OVER ME!
LUCKILY, SHUJI HASN'T HUNG OUT THE WASH YET, BUT I CAN'T FORGIVE THAT WITCH!
GRRRRRR
ME? I WAS ONLY WATERING MY PLANTS.
WHY WOULD I WATER YOUR HEAD, OLD MAN? NOTHING GROWS THERE.
SNAP
FUME

ARR
AA
AA
AA
SNAP
SNAP
LET ME AT HER!!
I'M WARNING YOU! CUT IT OUT!
GYAAAH
SHUT YOUR MOUTH, BOY!
GRP
GRP
LISTEN!
GRP
DON'T LET HER GET YOUR GOAT!
GRP
UGH!
SPLASH
HO HO
CLIK

SNAP
KERSPLASH
DON'T PULL THAT CRAP ON ME, YOU OLD BAG!
OH
OH
TOKINE! WHAT SHOULD WE DO?
LEAVE THEM ALONE. THEY'LL CALM DOWN SOONER OR LATER.
AH-CHOO!
YOU'RE A LOUDMOUTH EVEN WHEN YOU SNEEZE, GEEZER!
AARGH
AARGH
SQUIK
YOUR MEDDLING JUST MADE THINGS WORSE, BOY! NOW I'M SOAKED!

SCRUB
WHAT'S WITH YOU?
LAST NIGHT, YOU SEEMED TO BE GETTING ALONG WITH THE YUKIMURAS ...
SCRUB
I NEVER GET ALONG WITH THEM, STUPID!
MY BEAUTIFUL MUSTACHE IS RUINED...
SCRUB
BY THE WAY...
...WHAT'S THE SHADOW ORGANIZA-TION?

IS IT A CORPS OF DEMONS OR SOMETHING?
WHAT DO YOU MEAN BY THAT?
WELL, THEY LOOKED LIKE BAD GUYS TO ME.
AH. YES, THE NIGHT TROOPS ARE FULL OF RUFFIANS LIKE THE ONES WE SAW LAST NIGHT.
HOW CAN I PUT IT? THE SHADOW ORGANIZATION IS...
...AN ORGANIZATION OF THE SPECIALLY-TALENTED, BY THE SPECIALLY-TALENTED, FOR THE SPECIALLY-TALENTED.
...
I DON'T UNDERSTAND.
BROADLY SPEAKING, IT DOES TWO THINGS.
IT PROVIDES REGIONAL ORGANIZATION, AND IT HANDLES SECRET MATTERS.
BY SECRET MATTERS, DO YOU MEAN INCIDENTS WITH AYAKASHI?
SQUEAK
WELL, THEY DON'T RESTRICT THEMSELVES ONLY TO AYAKASHI.

IN THE OLD DAYS, WHEN THE DARKNESS WAS MORE PROFOUND, STRANGE EVENTS WERE COMMON.
TO COPE WITH THESE PHENOMENA, ORGANIZATIONS AROSE ACROSS JAPAN. THE MEMBERS WERE MAINLY PEOPLE ENDOWED WITH SPECIAL ABILITIES. THAT'S THE ORIGIN OF THE SHADOW ORGANIZATION.
TODAY, THE DIFFERENT REGIONS WORK IN CLOSER COOPERATION. ALSO, A CENTRAL HEADQUARTERS HAS BEEN CREATED TO SUPERVISE THE REGIONAL ACTIVITIES.

I SEE. SO THE ORGANIZATION ISN'T OUR ENEMY?
SHAKE
YOUR NAME IS REGISTERED IN THE SHADOW ORGANIZATION.
SQUEE
HUH?
WHY?
PING
EVERYONE KNOWN TO HAVE SPECIAL ABILITIES IS ON THEIR LIST, EVEN IF THEY DON'T BELONG TO THE ORGANIZATION.
LATELY, THE NUMBER OF AYAKASHI HAS BEEN DECREASING.
I HEAR IT'S GETTING HARDER TO ORGANIZE THE SPECIALLY-TALENTED.
SQUIK
SOME OF THEM HAVE MORE POWER THAN THEY CAN MANAGE.
ONE OF THE FUNCTIONS OF THE SHADOW ORGANIZATION IS TO GIVE THEM A PLACE TO BELONG TO AND AN OUTLET FOR THEIR TALENTS.
MAYBE YOU'RE TOO YOUNG TO UNDERSTAND THIS...
PAT PAT PAT PAT
ANYHOW, IT DOESN'T CONCERN YOU.
WHAT DO YOU MEAN, IT DOESN'T CONCERN ME?
AS A LEGITIMATE HEIR, YOU HAVE NOTHING TO DO WITH IT.

YOU SEE...
...THE SHADOW ORGANIZATION IS MADE UP OF MISFITS WHO AREN'T ENTITLED TO BECOME THE HEADS OF FAMILIES.
FATHER! YOSHIMORI! TOSHIMORI! BREAKFAST!

WSSSH
RATTLE
IT'S GETTING CHILLY.
OOO...
HUH ?
WONDER DOG
CHAK CHAK
SHP
MADARAO
HEY, TOSHI-MORI.
WHY DON'T YOU QUIT SERVING HER DOG FOOD?
WHY ?

SHE BELONGED TO OUR FOUNDING MASTER, DIDN'T SHE?
GRANDPA TOLD ME TO TREAT HER WELL.
TOSHI, DEMON DOGS DON'T EAT DOG FOOD.
I HAVEN'T GIVEN HER THAT DEER MEAT YET.
SO WHAT?
I'M TAKING CARE OF HER BECAUSE YOU DON'T.
AYAKASHI FEED ON PEOPLE'S CARE.
...
MADARAO IS A STRANGE DOG...
IT LOOKED LIKE SHE WAS INJURED BY THAT MONSTER LAST NIGHT, BUT I'M SURE SHE'S ALL RIGHT.
IN THE PAST, WHEN SHE WAS SWALLOWED BY ANOTHER AYAKASHI...
EEEK!
MADA-RAO!
GULP
MADA-RAO!
SLICE
SLICE
...I'D LOOK FOR HER IN VAIN.
THEN, THE NEXT DAY, SHE'D POP UP OUT OF HER HOUSE AS IF NOTHING HAD HAP-PENED.
YOU KNOW, I CAN NEVER GET USED TO DYING.
WHUP
WEREN'T YOU ALREADY DEAD?
AFTER EVERYTHING I WENT THROUGH...
...

TOKINE!
TOKINE!
DAK DAK DAK
TOKINE!
SHUT UP!
STAY AWAY FROM ME!
HEY!
HEY!
DID YOU KNOW OUR NAMES ARE REGISTERED WITH THE SHADOW ORGANIZATION?
...
YOU'RE FINALLY TAKING AN INTEREST IN THAT STUFF?
DIDN'T YOU KNOW THAT ALREADY?
WELL, SEEING THOSE GUYS LAST NIGHT...
...MADE ME CURIOUS.
I REALIZED THAT WE'RE SURROUNDED...
...BY A LOT OF MYSTERIES.
...

WHAT SEEMS THE MOST MYSTERIOUS IS THE KARASUMORI SITE.
...
IT SEEMS TO TREAT VARIOUS AYAKASHI DIFFER-ENTLY...
...WHEN IT FEEDS THEM POWER.
I DON'T THINK THE SITE AFFECTS ALL AYAKASHI IN THE SAME WAY, DO YOU?
LAST NIGHT'S MONSTER, FOR EXAMPLE...
DON'T GET TOO HUNG UP TRYING TO FIGURE IT OUT.
THAT SITE...
...IS MUCH MORE FRIGHTENING THAN YOU IMAGINE.

IS THAT SO?
YES.
...SO FAR...
...I'VE NEVER...
...BEEN AFRAID OF THE PLACE.

SUMI-MURA!
MMM?
I KNOW YOU'RE ALWAYS ASLEEP, BUT HAVE YOU NOTICED THE WEATHER? WHAT SEASON ARE WE IN NOW?
WHAT A STRANGE QUESTION.
IT'S AUTUMN NOW, RIGHT?
THIS IS THE THIRD AUTUMN WE'VE HAD THIS YEAR.
SHUK
THIS PLACE IS WEIRD ISN'T IT?
WHAT?
YEAH, AND HAVE YOU LOOKED BEHIND THE SCHOOL BUILDING?
YOU SEE?
RIGHT THERE.
THERE IS ONLY ONE THING I FEAR...

...AND THAT IS...
...SEEING SOMEONE I CARE FOR...
TOKINE!
TOKINE GOT...
...GET HURT RIGHT IN FRONT OF MY EYES.
THAT'S ALL I FEAR.
THIS REALLY IS A WEIRD PLACE.

YURI!
WOW.
AT MY SCHOOL, KARASUMORI ACADEMY...
...CHERRY BLOSSOMS ARE IN FULL BLOOM, BUT WINTER IS JUST AROUND THE CORNER.
Chapter 15: Cold Weather Cherry Blossoms (Part 1)
THE FLOWERS CAME ALL AT ONCE, EH?
I DIDN'T EVEN NOTICE.
STUDENTS HAVE HANDED DOWN, BY WORD OF MOUTH, THE 77 WONDERS OF KARASUMORI ACADEMY.
ONE OF THEM IS THE UNSEASONABLE BLOOMING OF CHERRY BLOSSOMS.
BUT I WONDER IF THEY'RE TRULY AWARE...
...THAT...
...THIS PLACE IS NOT NORMAL.
Yurina Kanda
Second Year, Class 2 of Karasumori Academy Junior High

THEN AGAIN...
...MAYBE "ABNORMAL" IS--
Chapter 15: COLD Weather Cherry BLOSSOMS (Part 1)
WHAT?
WHO'S THAT?
THAT'S NOT OUR SCHOOL UNIFORM.
IT'S REALLY OLD-FASHIONED...
HEY SUMIMURA, WHERE ARE YOU GOING?

CLASS IS STARTING!
DAK
DAK
DAK
ISN'T THAT A NICE IDEA, YURI?
HUH?
WHAT?
I SAID...
...HOW ABOUT BUYING A CAN OF JUICE AND HAVING A CHERRY-BLOSSOM VIEWING PARTY AT LUNCH?
UH... SURE.
HEY.
WHAT DO YOU MAKE OF THAT, KYOKO?
OF WHAT?
THERE, UNDER THE CHERRY TREE.
ON THE GROUND?
YOU MEAN THE TRASH?
WHAT AN ENVIRON-MENTALIST.
OH, SHOOT!
NO, NEVER MIND!
IT'S NOTHING.
...
I'D BETTER BE CAREFUL. I ALMOST SAID SOMETHING WEIRD AGAIN.
JUST AS I THOUGHT--SHE'S A GHOST.

WHY DO I SEE THESE THINGS?
TUK TUK
HUH?
?
WHAT'S HE DOING OVER THERE?
IT LOOKS LIKE...
...HE'S SAYING SOMETHING.
GRAB
WHAT?!
YURI! LET'S GET BACK TO CLASS!
THAT LOOKS LIKE SUMIMURA. HE'S IN MY CLASS.
NEXT, STARTING AT THE THIRD LINE ON PAGE 187...
WHY DON'T YOU READ THIS PART, IIDA?
SURE.
IT'S STRANGE.

HE'S ALWAYS SLEEP-ING.
HMM
AND I'VE ALWAYS THOUGHT HE SEEMED A LITTLE DIFFERENT FROM THE OTHER KIDS...
...
SUMI-MURA...
HE'S DEFINITELY STRANGE!
GLOOOOOM
I TOLD YOU TO GET OUT.
WHY'D YOU COME BACK?
I WANTED YOU TO LISTEN TO MY STORY...
DIDN'T I TELL YOU ABOUT THE COUNSEL-ING CENTER?
BUT I WANT YOU TO LISTEN TO MY STORY...
CAN YOU WAIT UNTIL AFTER CLASS?

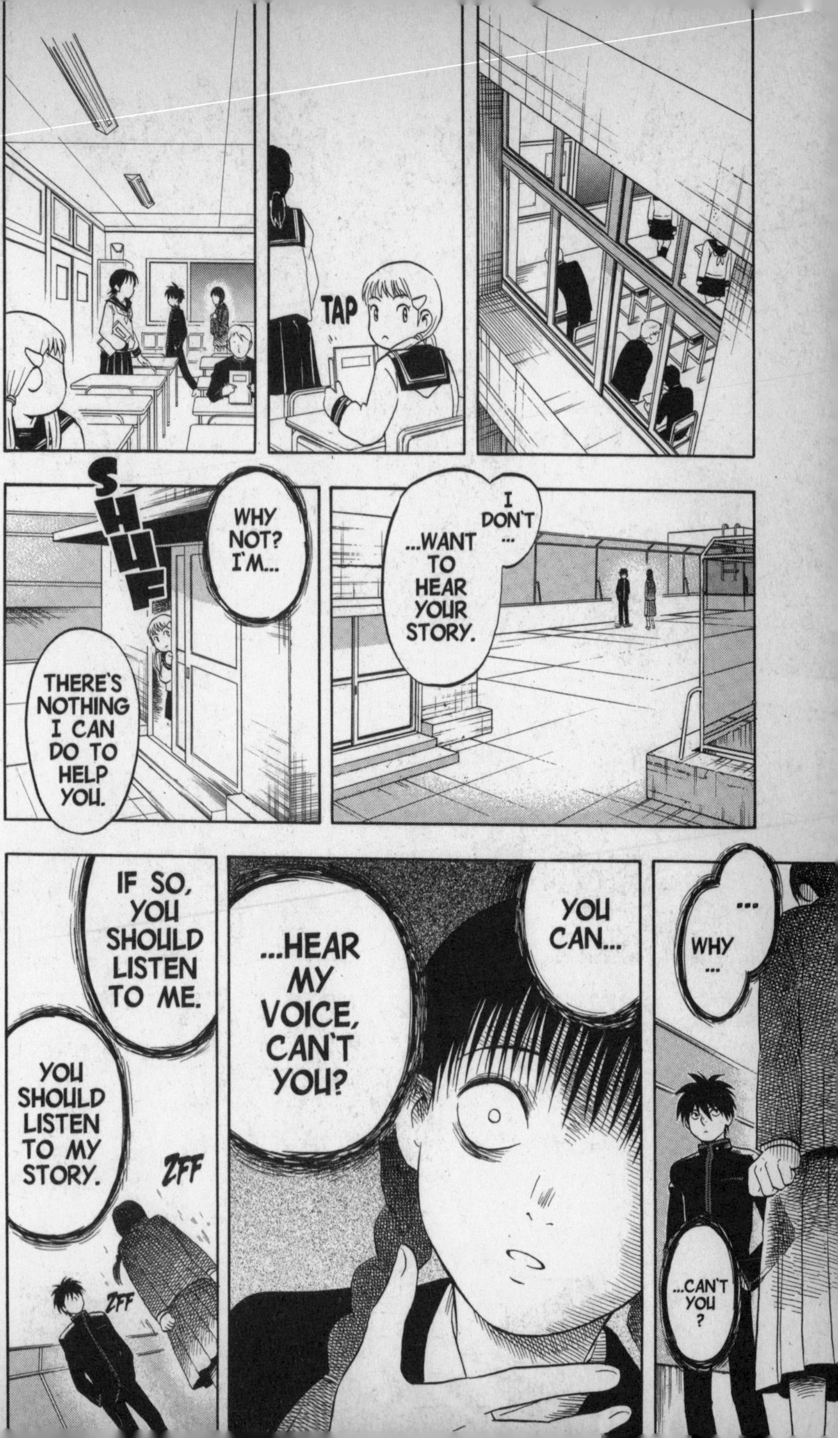
TAP
I DON'T ...
...WANT TO HEAR YOUR STORY.
SHUF
WHY NOT? I'M...
THERE'S NOTHING I CAN DO TO HELP YOU.
... WHY ...
...CAN'T YOU ?
YOU CAN...
...HEAR MY VOICE, CAN'T YOU?
IF SO, YOU SHOULD LISTEN TO ME.
YOU SHOULD LISTEN TO MY STORY.
ZFF
ZFF

ACTUALLY ... ...EVERYONE SHOULD LISTEN TO MY STORY...
RUMMMMMM
BLE
THAT'S RIGHT. EVERYONE SHOULD...
I SHOULD GET EVERYONE TO LISTEN TO ME...
WHIK
SQUIK
?!
UGH!
SQUIK SQUIK
GRR!
I HAVE NO CHOICE BUT TO TERMINATE YOU.
IF YOU'RE GOING TO ACT VIOLENTLY AT THIS PLACE...
...I WILL TERMINATE YOU IMMEDIATELY.
IF YOU DON'T WANT ME TO DO THAT, GET OUT OF HERE NOW.
WHAT ...

WHAT IS HE?
HE'S ...
...DANGEROUS.
HE TOLD THE GHOST HE'D "TERMINATE" HER.
JUST THEN, I GOT A CREEPY FEELING.
HE LOOKED LIKE A DEVIL.
I WONDER...
...IF HE'S EVEN HUMAN.
HMM
SCRITCH
SCRITCH
WOW!
WHAT NOW?
SCRITCH
SCRITCH
SCRITCH
HE'S REALLY INTENT ON WRITING SOMETHING!

HE SMILED!
GRIN
WHAT ...
WHAT'S THAT NOTEBOOK FOR?
I'M SORRY, KYOKO.
WHY DON'T YOU GO ON AHEAD?
YOU SURE, YURI?
I FORGOT SOMETHING.
SNEAK SNEAK
GOOD. NOBODY'S HERE.
THIS IS IT. THE DEVIL'S NOTEBOOK ...
SHUF
TOP SECRET
WHAAAH
SCRIBBLE
THE WRITING'S SO DENSE!
IT SAYS HERE, "SUGAR: 100 GRAMS." IS THIS SOME KIND OF CODE?

CHATTER CHATTER
COME TO THINK OF IT...
...HE SLEEPS ALL THE TIME, BUT PEOPLE ARE ALWAYS GATHERED AROUND HIM.
I WONDER IF HE HAS AN EVIL POWER THAT ATTRACTS PEOPLE...
OH!
TAK TAK
EVEN THE TEACHER IS DRAWN TO HIM!
THUD
SINCE YOU NEVER CAME TO MY OFFICE TO PICK THIS UP...
HEH
...I'M DELIVERING THIS SPECIAL PRESENT TO YOU WITH ADDITIONAL ASSIGNMENTS.
BOUND WITH A RIBBON.
A BRIBE?!
HURRY UP, YURI!
TAK TAK
WAIT FOR ME!

AW, MAN!
THE PLACE IS CRAWLING WITH HIGH-SCHOOL STUDENTS!
BUT THIS SITE BELONGS TO THE JUNIOR HIGH.
IT'S NOT FAIR! THE HIGH-SCHOOL STUDENTS BRING THEIR OWN LUNCHES. THEY CAN GET HERE FASTER.
HMM...
HMM. THOSE GIRLS ARE IN MY CLASS.
I'M SLEEPY.
WELL, WHY DON'T WE COME BACK WHEN THERE AREN'T SO MANY PEOPLE?
SLURP
BUBBLE
HOW ABOUT VIEWING THE CHERRY BLOSSOMS TONIGHT?
WHAT A GREAT IDEA!
OKAY, WE'LL MEET HERE AT MIDNIGHT.
WHAT?
BLUP
WHY...
...MID-NIGHT?
HEY, YOU!

WH-AH
DON'T EVER DO SUCH A FOOLISH THING!
THE SCHOOL IS DANGEROUS AT NIGHT!
COFFEE MILK
ESPECIALLY NEAR THE CHERRY TREE.
BYE.
TAK
TAK
WHAT WAS THAT?
GEEZ... WHO'S HE?
HE'S ONE OF OUR CLASS-MATES!
HEY.
DON'T YOU THINK HE'S STRANGE?
NO WAY.
WHAT?
HE'S NOT NORMAL AT ALL!
YOU SEE...
OH, NO, YURI.
IS THIS ANOTHER ONE OF YOUR MYSTICAL HUNCHES?

WHAT IS IT THIS TIME?
WHAT KIND OF EVIL SPIRIT IS HE POSSESSED BY?
TELL ME, TELL ME.
HUH? OH!
I'M NOT ...
I'M NOT SAYING HE'S...
NO.
I SHOULDN'T TELL THEM ABOUT HIM.
IF I DO...
...THEY'LL THINK I'M...
IT'LL BE MID-NIGHT SOON...
I WONDER WHY THESE CHERRY BLOSSOMS KEEP BLOOMING OVER AND OVER.
OUR LORD LOVED CHERRY BLOSSOMS.
IS THAT SO?
"CRAZY CHERRY BLOSSOMS," RIGHT?

THAT'S THE OLD SAYING. THEY'RE SUPPOSED TO DRIVE PEOPLE CRAZY.
THATS RIGHT.
LORD TOKIMORI USED TO SAY THAT.
OUR FOUNDING MASTER SAID THAT?
CHERRY BLOSSOMS MAKE THOSE WHO VIEW THEM VERY HAPPY.
AFTER SEEING THEM, PEOPLE GET ALL EXCITED.
AND...
...ACCORDING TO LORD TOKIMORI ...
...THAT'S THE KEY FEATURE OF THIS SITE.
KEY FEATURE?
AYANO! KYOKO!

I'M SORRY.
TROT
TROT
I'M LATE--HUH?
SCRITCH SCRITCH
IT'S HIM!
IT'S...
...
OH, NO!
EEEK
I THOUGHT YOU WERE SOMEONE ELSE--
...THAT ...
SQUEEZE
I'LL TERMINATE YOU!
WAHAHAHAHA
...DANGEROUS BOY!
SHUK
GASP

GO HOME.
WHAT ?
WHY ...
...ARE YOU BEING SO RUDE?
JUST GO HOME, IT'S DANGEROUS HERE.
EX-EXCUSE ME, BUT...
...I'M SUPPOSED TO MEET SOMEONE HERE.
IF YOU'RE TALKING ABOUT THE TWO GIRLS, I'VE ALREADY SENT THEM HOME.
WHAAAT ?!
WHAT... WHAT DID YOU DO TO THEM?
SOB
SOB
SOB
ARE...ARE THEY STILL ALIVE?
WHAT ?
OF COURSE.
WHAT'S WRONG WITH THIS GIRL?
YOSHIMORI.

WHAT DO YOU PLAN TO DO WITH THIS GIRL...
...AT NIGHT UNDER THE CHERRY BLOSSOMS?
ER...
I DIDN'T THINK SHE'D SHOW UP.
LOOKS LIKE YOU GUESSED WRONG.
OH, SHUT UP.
WAAH
THERE'S ANOTHER ONE LIKE HIM...
ANYWAY, KANDA.
YAUGH!
PAT
YOU'D BETTER HURRY UP AND GO HO--
CHIK
HERE THEY COME!
RUSTLE
CRUD!
RUSTLE
?
COME ON! THIS WAY!
GRAB
UGH!

STAY HERE AND DON'T MOVE!
WHAT ?
WHAT ?
GOT IT?
HEY.
IS IT OKAY FOR HER TO SEE US AT WORK ?
A NORMAL PERSON CAN'T SEE ANYTHING ANYWAY. LET'S FINISH OUR JOB.
HERE THEY COME...
...MY FAVORITE CHERRY-BLOSSOM VIEWERS!
CHK
WHOOOOOOSH
WHAT ...
WHAT THE HECK IS THAT ?!
EEK!

Chapter 16: Cold Weather Cherry Blossoms (Part 2)

CHAPTER 16
COLD WEATHER CHERRY
BLOSSOMS (PART 2)
...WHAT
THE HECK
ARE THOSE
THINGS
?!

WHOOSH

HOI!
JOSO!
WH
OO
OO
VUM
ZT ZT ZT ZT ZT
KETSU!!
WHAAAAMMM
MMM

TOO MUCH ENERGY, AS USUAL!
IT'S FASTER THIS WAY!
FWASH
KETSU!
WHAM
WHAM
KETSU!
WHAM
WHAM
WHAM
KETSU!
WHAM
WHAM
YOU SEE? A LOT OF THEM SLIP RIGHT OUT.
SHUT UP.

BAM
BAM
BAM
BOOM
METSU!!
WHOOOO
CRUD!
HERE COME SOME MORE...
WHO ARE THESE PEOPLE?
YAAUGH
WHAT DID THEY JUST DO?

GASP
TAP
TAP
TAP
HYA HYA HYA
EEK!
CHOMP
EEP!
...
MUNCH
MUNCH
CHIK
GULP
SHOO
HMPH.

HEY, MADA-RAO!
WHAT ARE YOU DOING?
I'M WORKING HERE.
CHOMP
MY ONLY PLEASURE COMES FROM EATING THE PIPSQUEAKS THAT FALL UNDER THE INFLUENCE OF THE CHERRY BLOSSOMS.
WA
HA HA
PRETTY TASTY!
THIS ISN'T THE BEST TIME TO LET YOURSELF BE AFFECTED BY THE BLOSSOMS.
WE'RE ONLY FIGHTING SMALL FRIES TONIGHT.
HAKUBI.
STOP EATING THEM.
HM.
HYUK
FLOP
FLOP
HYUK
HYUK
METSU!
BOO
...
HMPH.
WAAAAAAA
I'M FED UP WITH THEM.
AAH

TOKINE!
WILL YOU FINISH UP AROUND HERE?
WHAT?
HOI!
WHPP
JOSO!
ZK ZK ZK ZK ZK ZK ZK ZK
KETSU!!
WHAAAAAM
HEY, YOSHI-MORI!

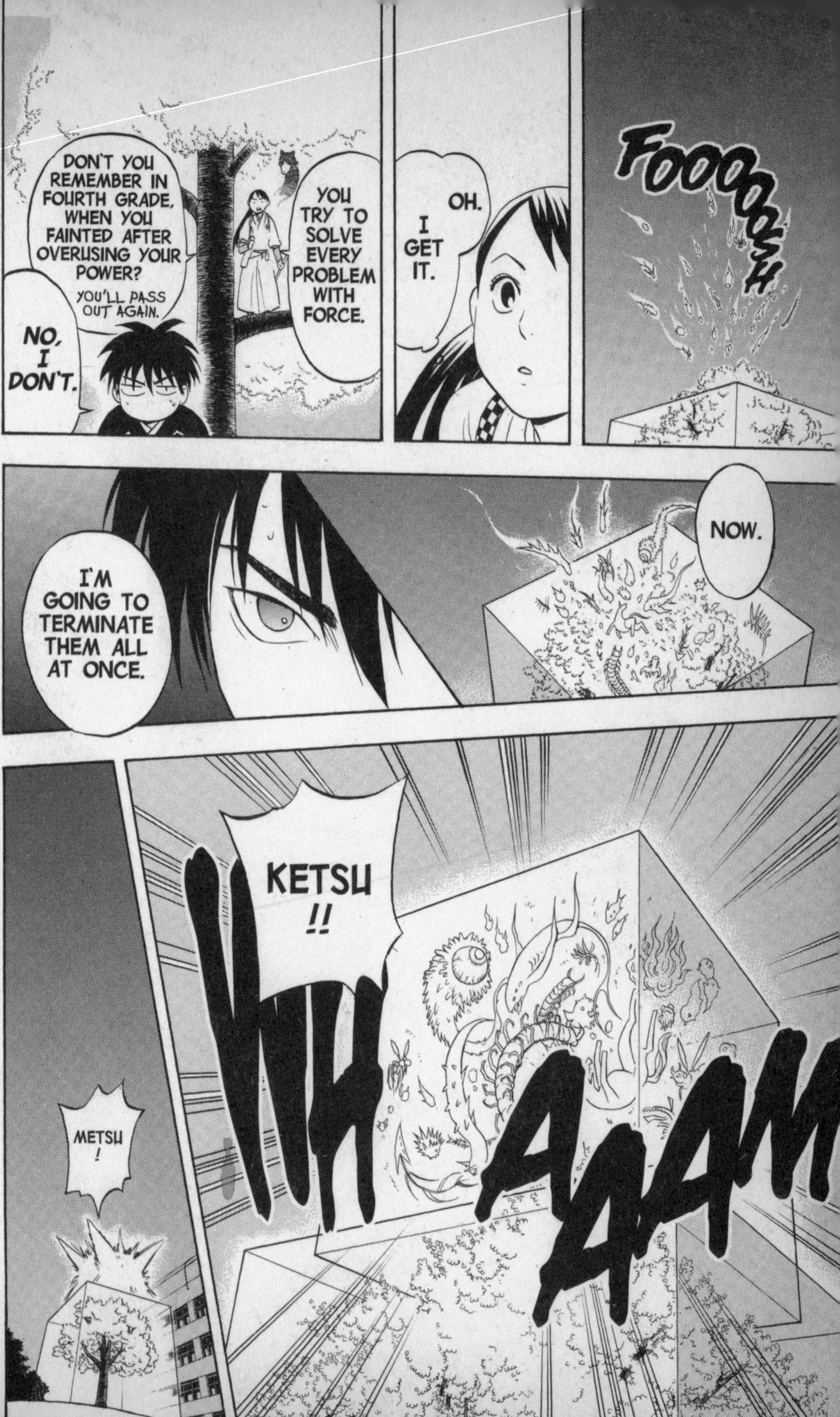
FOOOOOSH
OH. I GET IT.
YOU TRY TO SOLVE EVERY PROBLEM WITH FORCE.
DON'T YOU REMEMBER IN FOURTH GRADE, WHEN YOU FAINTED AFTER OVERUSING YOUR POWER?
YOU'LL PASS OUT AGAIN.
NO, I DON'T.
NOW.
I'M GOING TO TERMINATE THEM ALL AT ONCE.
KETSU !!
WHAAAM
METSU !

ARE WE DONE YET?
NOT AS LONG AS THE CHERRY BLOSOMS ARE IN BLOOM.
SHATUK
HOW ABOUT ELIMINATING THE CHERRY BLOSSOMS?
NO.
THIS CHERRY TREE IS ABLE TO BLOOM AS MANY TIMES AS IT WANTS.
WHAT...
WHAT SHOULD I DO?
THEY KEPT FORMING AND SMASHING THOSE SQUARE THINGS, OVER AND OVER AGAIN.
BUT STILL—
AND I'M...
...INSIDE A SQUARE THING.
OH.
I FORGOT.

KANDA?
SHF
HE'S...
HE'S GOING TO KILL ME!!
PLIP
PLIP
PLIP
YOU CAN MOVE NOW.
HEY, WHAT'S THE MATTER?
WHA?
EEK!
EEK!
OH, DEAR! YOU MADE HER CRY!
TEE HEE
I'M SORRY.
HEH
THIS IDIOT WAS TOO ROUGH, WASN'T HE?
EEEE!
...!!

THAT'S WHAT I THOUGHT.
SHOOO
EEK!
SNIF
SNIF
SHE'S SCARED OF YOU.
SHUT UP. YOU TAKE CARE OF HER.
WHAAAAAAT?!
WHAT?
THIS GIRL HAS SPECIAL ABILITIES.
I MEAN SHE CAN SEE THINGS.
UM...
KANDA?
IDIOT.
...

BAM
I'M SORRY!
I'M REALLY SORRY!
I DIDN'T KNOW YOU COULD SEE!
I DIDN'T MEAN TO FRIGHTEN YOU.
THIS MAY SOUND LIKE AN EXCUSE, BUT...
...LET ME EXPLAIN A FEW THINGS TO YOU.
...
WELL... THIS JOB IS...
HE LOOKS ...
ER...
LET ME GIVE YOU AN EX-AMPLE ...
WHAT ?
NO, THAT WOULDN'T HELP YOU UNDERSTAND...
...DIFFERENT NOW.

HE LOOKS LIKE AN ORDINARY BOY.
I'M SORRY.
I KNOW IT'S ASKING A LOT AFTER ALL THIS, BUT...
...CAN YOU PLEASE KEEP WHAT YOU SAW TONIGHT SECRET?
I'M NOT GOING TO TELL ANYONE. THEY'LL JUST THINK I'M CRAZY.
HA HA HA
THAT'S TRUE.
I WONDER IF...
...HE DOESN'T MIND...
HEY... DON'T YOU MIND...
...HAVING SUCH A STRANGE POWER?
HUH?
NOT REALLY.
WELL...
I USED TO HATE MY FAMILY BUSINESS.

BUT THINGS THAT MUST SEEM STRANGE TO OTHER PEOPLE...
...HAVE COME TO SEEM NORMAL TO ME.
NORMAL?
I DON'T MIND HAVING THIS POWER ANYMORE.
I SEE.
IMPRESSIVE.
HUH?
IMPRESSIVE?
ANYWAY...
I HAVE MORE WORK TO DO, SO I CAN'T WALK YOU HOME.
WILL YOU KEEP THIS SECRET, TOO?
PING
HE'S REALLY WEIRD.
HEE HEE!

BUT I'M...
...WEIRD, TOO.
HEE HEE
WHY DO I FEEL SO HAPPY NOW?
CAN YOU WALK A LITTLE FASTER?
OH.
THAT'S MY HOUSE.
THANK YOU FOR WALKING ME HOME.
POOF
FWAP
THE NEXT DAY...
...THE CHERRY BLOSSOMS WERE COMPLETELY GONE.
BUT...
...IT'S NORMAL FOR A TREE TO BE BARE AT THIS TIME OF THE YEAR.
FUMBLE
YURI!

WHY DIDN'T YOU SHOW UP LAST NIGHT?!
WE SAW THE WEIRDEST THING!
A LONG-HAIRED MAN WITH A ROSE IN HIS MOUTH WAS SPINNING LIKE A TOP!
AND HE SMILED AND WINKED AT US!
WINK
WE WERE SCARED
ALTHOUGH I SAW MUCH STRANGER STUFF...
...I'M GOING TO KEEP IT SECRET.

AN EXTRA PIECE OF MANGA
MORE BEHIND-THE-SCENES STORIES
PART I: ABOUT THE CHARACTERS
SOME OF MY READERS MAY ALREADY KNOW THIS, BUT "KEKKAISHI" WAS PUBLISHED AS TWO SELF-CONTAINED SHORT STORIES BEFORE IT WAS INTRODUCED AS A SERIES.
ONE STORY APPEARED IN A WEEKLY MAGAZINE, AND THE OTHER IN A SPECIAL ISSUE OF ANOTHER MAGAZINE.
THEY WERE BOTH A BIT DIFFERENT FROM THE CURRENT SERIES.
BECAUSE I'D ALREADY WRITTEN THOSE STORIES, THE EARLY DISCUSSIONS WITH MY EDITOR ABOUT THE SERIES WENT RELATIVELY SMOOTHLY. HOWEVER...
AFTER THE SHORT STORY WAS PUBLISHED IN THE WEEKLY MAGAZINE...
REGARDING THE RENDERING OF THE MAIN CHARACTERS...
EDITOR-IN-CHIEF (SIZE: GIANT)
TANABE (SIZE: SMALL)
I WAS ASKED...
...TO MAKE THEM PRETTIER.
WAAAH
DOES THAT MEAN...
...YOU THINK THE CURRENT CHARACTERS AREN'T PRETTY?!
I KNOW THEY'RE NOT TRENDY TYPES.
NOOO NOOO
BUT... BUT...
PERSON-ALLY, I THINK THEY LOOK JUST FINE NOW, BUT THE OTHER EDITORS...
ANYWAY, WHY DON'T YOU TRY OUT SOME NEW IDEAS..
...INCLUD-ING SOME LOOKS YOU DON'T THINK YOU LIKE?
OKAY...
I TOOK THIS AS AN OPPORTUNITY TO EXPLORE DIFFERENT FACES. I CAME UP WITH SOME NEW DESIGNS.
HOW'S THIS?
HA!
I GET WORKED UP EASILY.

HOW DO YOU LIKE THESE LOOKS FOR THE HERO?

(DESIGNS FOR YOSHIMORI)

THIS IS CLOSE TO THE WAY I DRAW HIM NOW. AFTER ADDING A TWINKLE IN THE EYES, WE DECIDED TO GO WITH THIS DESIGN.

A TYPICAL LOOK FOR A MANGA HERO. IT DOESN'T LOOK LIKE A GUY WHO'D MAKE CASTLE CAKES, THOUGH.

I USED THIS FACE FOR THE HERO IN A DIFFERENT STORY. DOESN'T HE LOOK LIKE A JUVENILE DELINQUENT, THOUGH?

HERE I TRIED TO GIVE HIM AN UNUSUAL LOOK. HE LOOKS LIKE HE CAN'T BE EXPOSED TO SUNLIGHT.

THIS IS A CUTESY LITTLE TYPE. TOO MUCH LIKE AN ANIME CHARACTER, HUH?

I DON'T LIKE AN EIGHTH-GRADER TO LOOK AS SAVAGE AS THIS.

DOESN'T THIS LOOK LIKE A CHARACTER IN AN OLD-TIMEY ANIME? IT HAS KIND OF A RETRO APPEAL. THE SIDEBURNS WOULD BE REVIVED LATER IN THE SERIES.

THIS DESIGN WOULD DEFINITELY BE FOR YOUNGER READERS THAN OUR TARGET AUDIENCE. HE LOOKS LIKE THE SORT OF ANIME CHARACTER WHO TRAVELS TO OTHER WORLDS.

HOW DO YOU LIKE THESE LOOKS FOR THE HEROINE?
(DESIGNS FOR TOKINE)

THIS IS THE CLOSEST DESIGN TO THE ONE I CURRENTLY USE. I ENDED UP MAKING TOKINE LOOK A LITTLE OLDER THAN THIS.

THIS HAS THE LOOK OF AN OLD CHILDHOOD FRIEND, DOESN'T IT? THIS WAS A STRONG POSSIBILITY FOR TOKINE.

THIS HAS THE LOOK OF A GOOD GIRL FROM A TRADITIONAL FAMILY. SHE RADIATES TRADITION AND FORMALITY.

I PERSONALLY THINK THIS ONE LOOKS TOO YOUNG, BUT IT COULD BE A POSSIBLE CHOICE. SHE DOESN'T LOOK OLDER THAN YOSHIMORI AT ALL, THOUGH.

THIS IS A DESIGN YOU'D OFTEN FIND IN OLD ANIME. MY EDITOR TOLD ME THAT SHE LOOKS LIKE A WOMAN IN AN OLD-FASHIONED EROTIC MANGA. DO YOU THINK SO?

THIS IS A "RETRO GIRLY" STYL (WHATEVER THAT MEANS). YO DON'T USUALLY FIND THIS TYP IN BOYS' MANGA, THOUGH.

IN AMERICAN COMIC BOOKS, YOU SEE THIS TYPE VERY OFTEN. HOWEVER, SHE MIGHT LOOK TOO GROWN-UP FOR TOKINE'S CHARACTER.

THIS ONE IS ABSOLUTELY NOT FOR BOYS' MANGA. SHE'D BE TOO MUCH FOR YOSHIMORI TO HANDLE. DOESN'T THIS GIRL LOOK VERY JAPANESE, THOUGH?

I CAME UP WITH MANY OTHER POSSIBILITIES. AFTER ALL THAT...
YOUR PLAN WORKED. WE'VE DECIDED, FOR THE MOST PART, TO KEEP THE CURRENT DESIGNS FOR THE CHARACTERS.
THE OTHER CHOICES DON'T WORK.
I SEE...
I THOUGHT THEY WERE INTER-ESTING OPTIONS...
WHY WON'T YOU BELIEVE I WAS REALLY TRYING?
...WE DECIDED NOT TO MAKE MAJOR CHANGES IN THE CHARACTER DESIGNS.
WHAMM
METSUU!
WHAMM
WAIT A MINUTE, YOSHIMORI!
SWOOSH
I'M GLAD THESE SCENES NEVER CAME TO PASS.
YOSHIMORI SUMIMURA, 14, IS THE DEDICATED SUCCESSOR TO A KEKKAISHI FAMILY WITH A 400-YEAR HISTORY. HE DOESN'T WANT TO TAKE OVER THE FAMILY BUSINESS, BUT HE WORKS AT NIGHT TO ERADICATE AYAKASHI AND PROTECT HIS FRIEND, TOKINE.
WHAT DO YOU THINK, READERS?
結界師
(KEKKAISHI)
田辺イエロウ
(YELLOW TANABE)
I DREW THIS PICTURE TO BE USED AS AN AD POSTER AT BOOKSTORES.

PART 2: ABOUT THE KEKKAISHI MAGIC
THE CONCEPT OF THE "KEKKAI" (PROTECTIVE WARD) HAS EXISTED IN JAPAN SINCE ANCIENT TIMES.
I CREATED THE TERM.
NORMALLY, A KEKKAI IS CONSIDERED SOMETHING LIKE A BARRIER OR SHIELD...
...THAT PROTECTS A PERSON OR ENCLOSES UNWANTED OBJECTS.
COO COO
HE'S DEFENDING HIMSELF.
HOW-EVER...
CAN'T WE FIGHT A BATTLE USING KEKKAI?
...AFTER HAVING THIS THOUGHT, I CAME UP WITH THE IDEA OF USING KEKKAI OFFENSIVELY AS WELL AS DEFENSIVELY.
THERE I CHOSE MY FAVORITE CUBIC AND RECTANGULAR PARALLELE-PIPED SHAPES FOR MY KEKKAI.
SHING
THE SHAPE IS SIMPLE AND PRACTICAL.
ALTHOUGH NOT TOO EXOTIC.
AFTER DETERMINING THE SHAPE OF THE KEKKAI, I INVENTED THE FOLLOWING KEKKAI MECHANISM.
"HOI" DESIGNATES THE TARGET.
VMM
"JOSO" DETERMINES THE LOCATION.
ZK
ZK
"KETSU" FORMS AND ACTIVATES A KEKKAI SHIELD.
WHAM
I NAMED EACH STEP ACCORDINGLY.
THE PROCEDURE RESEMBLES THE METHOD OF DRAWING A THREE-DIMENSIONAL SHAPE: LENGTH, WIDTH, AND HEIGHT.

SO...
METSU!
BOOM
...ONE CAN DESTROY AN OPPONENT BY SMASHING THE KEKKAI. OR, OF COURSE...
I'M SORRY.
KAI.
WHOOSH
...ONE CAN CHOOSE A PEACEFUL SOLUTION BY CANCELING THE KEKKAI.
IT'S VERY SIMPLE MAGIC, BUT CAN BE APPLIED TO MANY DIFFERENT SITUATIONS.
IF I COULD USE THIS MAGIC IN REAL LIFE, IT WOULD BE VERY CONVENIENT.
I WOULDN'T NEED SARAN WRAP ANYMORE.
IT'S TRANSPARENT AND HAS A COOL LOOK.
I'D MAKE A TV TABLE.
CAN YOU COME UP WITH BETTER USES?
I WISH I COULD MASTER THIS SORT OF MAGIC.
KEKKAI JUTSU IS VERY PRACTICAL MAGIC, USEFUL BOTH IN COMBAT AND IN DAILY LIVING.
HA!
WHAM!
PROBABLY BECAUSE OF THIS QUALITY, THE CHARACTERS OFTEN LOSE SIGHT OF THE BORDER BETWEEN THEIR DAILY LIVES AND THEIR BATTLES WITH AYAKASHI.

WATERING THE PLANTS WITH A WATER BOTTLE THAT SHOULD BE USED FOR MY PAINTS.

MESSAGE FROM YELLOW TANABE

On the morning Kekkaishi Volume One went on sale, a pot of orchids was delivered to my house. It was a gift from a relative of mine, celebrating the title's release.

I was caught unprepared for such a thing and screamed, "It's…it's orchids!!"

Later, another flower shop phoned to tell me that they were delivering flowers to my house. The sender's name was unfamiliar to me. As I waited nervously, the flowers arrived. I screamed, "Orchids again!" It turned out to be another relative of mine (whom I don't know) sending more orchids.

Thank you, everyone.

KEKKAISHI

VOLUME 2

STORY AND ART BY YELLOW TANABE

English Adaptation/Shaenon Garrity
Translation/Yuko Sawada
Touch-up Art & Lettering/Stephen Dutro
Cover Design & Graphic Layout/Amy Martin
Editors/Eric Searleman & Megan Bates

Managing Editor/Annette Roman
Director of Production/Noboru Watanabe
Vice President of Publishing/Alvin Lu
Sr. Director of Acquisitions/Rika Inouye
Vice President of Sales & Marketing/Liza Coppola
Publisher/Hyoe Narita

Printed in Canada

Published by VIZ, LLC
P.O. Box 77010
San Francisco, CA 94107

Action Edition
10 9 8 7 6 5 4 3 2 1
First printing, July 2005

Editor's Recommendations

MÄR

Ginta Toramizu is a 14-year-old kid who doesn't have a lot going for him: he's near-sighted, doesn't do well in school, sucks at sports, and to top it off—he's short! Then one day a supernatural figure appears at his school and summons him to a mysterious and exciting new world! In this strange universe filled with magic and wonder, he is strong, tough, agile—and he can see without his glasses! Thus, Ginta begins a mystical quest in search of the magical items known as "ÄRMS," with his companions Jack and the talking iron-ball weapon known as "Babbo."

Fullmetal Alchemist

In an alchemical ritual gone wrong, Edward Elric lost his leg. He was lucky...his brother Alphonse lost his entire body. At the cost of his arm, Edward was able to rescue his brother's soul and preserve it in a suit of steel armor. Equipped with mechanical "auto-mail" limbs, Edward becomes a state alchemist, serving the government on deadly missions and seeking the one thing that can restore his and his brother's bodies...the legendary Philosopher's Stone.

Excel Saga

Today the city—tomorrow, the world! That's the plan of Il Palazzo, the haughty leader of ACROSS, a secret society based somewhere deep beneath the streets and sewers of Fukuoka, Japan. It's a good thing he's starting small, because ACROSS begins its bid for global domination with just two members—Il Palazzo and Excel, the teenaged girl smitten with him.

A Zero Becomes A Hero
Ginta's near-sighted, clumsy and short...
but things are about to change!
When you're a loser, you often dream about the day you're anything but. For Ginta, that day has come—now he's in a fantasy world where he has all the abilities he lacks in real life. This world is also full of magical items, one of which may have the power to send him home. But will Ginta want to go?
Get drawn into Ginta's journey with graphic novels —now available at store.viz.com!
ONLY $7.99!
MÄR
MÄRCHEN AWAKENS ROMANCE
Nobuyuki Anzai
Vol. 1
viz media
www.viz.com
store.viz.com
© 2003 Nobuyuki Anzai/Shogakukan, Inc.

Prepare For Battle!
Tyson is a boy with a passion for Beyblades. His enemies are the militant Blade Sharks, who want to win at any cost! Can Tyson get the skills and training to beat them in a Beyblade battle?
From the JETIX anime series and the popular HASBRO toys — start your graphic novel collection today!
Only $7.99!
action
BEYBLADE
Vol. 1
Story and art by Takao Aoki
BEYBLADE™
© 2000 Takao Aoki/Shogakukan, Inc.
© 2000 HUDSON SOFT/TAKARA
Logo and graphics © HUDSON SOFT/TAKARA•BEYBLADE PROJECT• TV TOKYO. Licensed by d-rights Inc.
www.viz.com
store.viz.com
viz media

Without a Past?
From the original manga artist of SPRIGGAN—get armed with the manga and anime today!
プロジェクトアームズ
PROJECT ARMS
PROJECT ARMS
The 2nd Chapter
Anime only $24.98
DVD VIDEO
viz media
www.viz.com
store.viz.com
©Ryoji Minagawa • Kyoichi Nanatsuki/Shogakukan • TV Tokyo • TMS

How many manga titles have you purchased in the last year? How many were VIZ titles?
(please check one from each column)

MANGA	VIZ
☐ None	☐ None
☐ 1 – 4	☐ 1 – 4
☐ 5 – 10	☐ 5 – 10
☐ 11+	☐ 11+

How much influence do special promotions and gifts-with-purchase have on the titles you buy?
(please circle, with 5 being great influence and 1 being none)

1 2 3 4 5

Do you purchase every volume of your favorite series?

☐ Yes! Gotta have 'em as my own ☐ No. Please explain: ______________________

What kind of manga storylines do you most enjoy? **(check all that apply)**

☐ Action / Adventure ☐ Science Fiction ☐ Horror
☐ Comedy ☐ Romance (shojo) ☐ Fantasy (shojo)
☐ Fighting ☐ Sports ☐ Historical
☐ Artistic / Alternative ☐ Other ______________________

If you watch the anime or play a video or TCG game from a series, how likely are you to buy the manga? **(please circle, with 5 being very likely and 1 being unlikely)**

1 2 3 4 5

If unlikely, please explain: ______________________

Who are your favorite authors / artists? ______________________

____

What titles would like you translated and sold in English? ______________________

____

THANK YOU! Please send the completed form to:

VIZ media

NJW Research
42 Catharine Street
Poughkeepsie, NY 12601

Your privacy is very important to us. All information provided will be used for internal purposes only and will not be sold or otherwise divulged.